My Wedding
Remembered

Written by
Kimberly Hertlein

Illustrated by
Deb Mores

Crown Publishers, Inc.   New York

To my mother and mother-in-law
for making my wedding
a day I will always remember.
K. A. H

Published by Crown Publishers, Inc.
201 East 50th Street, New York, New York 10022
Member of the Crown Publishing Group.

Random House, Inc. New York, Toronto, London,
Sydney, Auckland.

CROWN is a trademark of Crown Publishers, Inc.

Manufactured in Singapore

ISBN 0-517-59907-4

10 9 8 7 6 5 4 3 2 1

First Edition

Bride

Groom

Wedding Date

Our *Life* as It Became

We met _____

_____

_____

_____

_____

_____

_____

What attracted me to you (and you to me) _____

_____

_____

_____

_____

_____

_____

_____

Our friendship grew and _____

_____

_____

_____

_____

_____

_____

I remember our first kiss _____
_____
_____
_____
_____
_____

I began to fall in love with you (and you with me) _____
_____
_____
_____
_____
_____
_____
_____

I knew I wanted to spend the rest of my life with you (and you with me) _____
_____
_____
_____
_____

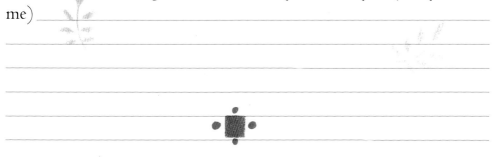

Our Lives Examined

What drives us and motivates us to be who we are? _____

_____

_____

_____

_____

_____

_____

_____

_____

What do we both feel passionate about? _____

_____

_____

_____

_____

_____

_____

_____

_____

_____

What do we want from life, from ourselves, and from and for each other?

The Life We Share

What we enjoy doing together _____
_____
_____
_____

What we have in common _____
_____
_____
_____

What we don't have in common _____
_____
_____
_____

Your presence in my life has inspired/encouraged/motivated
me to (and you to) _____
_____
_____
_____
_____

The best times we've shared _____

_____

_____

_____

_____

_____

And the most difficult times we've shared _____

_____

_____

_____

_____

_____

_____

Our most romantic/sensual/sentimental times together _____

_____

_____

_____

_____

_____

The World in the Year of Our Wedding

Who was president? _____

Who was vice-president? _____

Who was governor/mayor? _____

Most popular books _____

_____

Most popular songs _____

_____

Most popular movies _____

_____

Most popular fashions _____

_____

Most popular political personalities _____

_____

_____

Most popular celebrities _____

_____

_____

The topics/issues of the day _____

_____

The $\mathcal{H}$onor of Your Hand

How was the subject of marriage brought up? _____ _____
_____
_____
_____

How long did we think and talk about getting married? _____
_____
_____

And why? _____
_____
_____
_____

Who said to whom, "Will you marry me?" _____

What was the date? _____

Were there any special circumstances surrounding this date? _____
_____ _____
_____
_____

Did we do anything special to celebrate? _____
_____
_____

All About the Bride

Bride's full name _____

Date of birth _____

Place of birth _____

Mother's full name _____

Father's full name _____

Sisters/brothers _____

_____

_____

Maternal grandmother's name _____

Maternal grandfather's name _____

Paternal grandmother's name _____

Paternal grandfather's name _____

Education _____

_____

_____

Occupation _____

_____

Special interests _____

_____

_____

All About the *Bride's* Family

Where did my mother's family come from? _____

_____

_____

Where did my father's family come from? _____

_____

_____

My parents were married on _____

at _____

in _____

They were _____ years old.

My most memorable times with them _____

_____

_____

_____

_____

_____

_____

_____

_____

_____

_____

_____

All About the Groom

Groom's full name _____

Date of birth _____

Place of birth _____

Mother's full name _____

Father's full name _____

Sisters/brothers _____
_____

Maternal grandmother's name _____

Maternal grandfather's name _____

Paternal grandmother's name _____

Paternal grandfather's name _____

Education _____
_____
_____

Occupation _____
_____

Special interests _____
_____
_____

All About the *Groom's* Family

Where did his mother's family come from? _____

_____

Where did his father's family come from? _____

_____

His parents were married on _____

at _____

in _____

They were _____ years old.

My most memorable times with them _____

_____

_____

_____

_____

_____

_____

_____

_____

_____

_____

_____

_____

_____

The Engagement

Family celebrations _____

_____

_____

_____

_____

Engagement parties _____

_____

_____

_____

Special gifts/tokens _____

_____

_____

_____

_____

_____

_____

_____

(Draw/or place photo
of ring here.)

Engagement Announcements

(Place announcements here.)

The $\mathcal{P}$lanning

We decided to have the wedding on _____

at _____

in _____

Who did we ask to perform the ceremony? _____

_____

_____

Who did I ask to be my maid of honor/matron of honor and attendants? _____

_____

_____

_____

Who did my fiancé ask to be his best man and ushers? _____

_____

_____

_____

_____

Who did we ask to be the flower girl
and/or ring bearer _____

_____

_____

_____

Parties/Showers

You Are Invited

Date _____

Time _____

Place _____

Given by _____

_____

Special gifts/tokens _____

_____

_____

_____

You Are Invited

Date _____

Time _____

Place _____

Given by _____

_____

Special gifts/tokens _____

_____

_____

_____

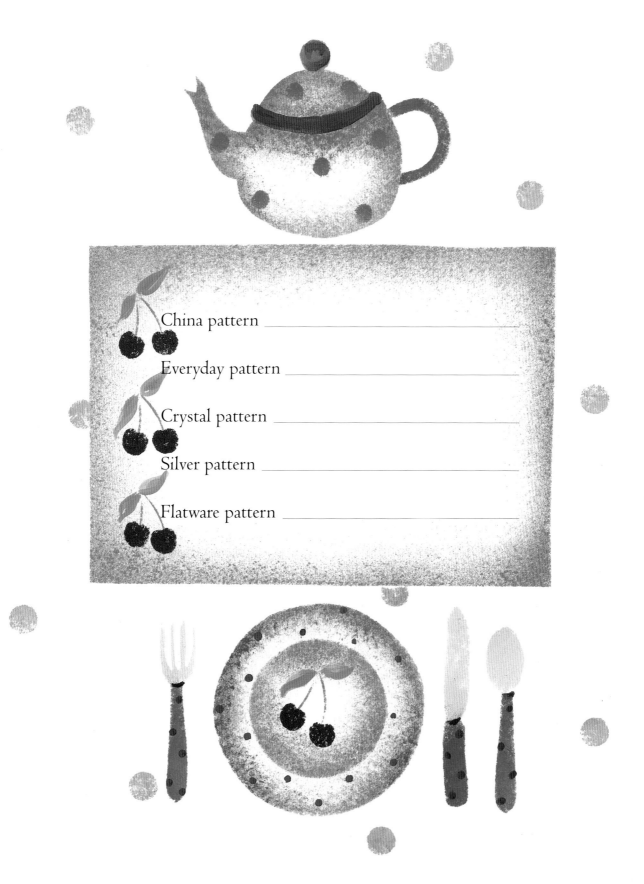

China pattern _____

Everyday pattern _____

Crystal pattern _____

Silver pattern _____

Flatware pattern _____

Something Old, Something New, Something Borrowed, Something Blue

My dress was _____

_____

_____

My veil was _____

_____

_____

My accessories were _____

_____

_____

My something old, something new, something borrowed, something blue was _____

_____

_____

_____

I carried _____

_____

_____

The attendants' dresses were _____

_____

_____

_____

_____

_____

I picked the color because _____

_____

_____

_____

Their accessories (headpieces, jewelry) were _____

_____

_____

_____

_____

They carried _____

_____

_____

_____

_____

The groom wore _____

_____

_____

_____

_____

_____

The ushers wore _____

_____

_____

_____

_____

_____

The boutonnieres were _____

_____

_____

The flower girl and/or ring bearer wore _____

_____

_____

_____

She and/or he carried _____
_____
_____
_____
_____

My mother wore _____
_____
_____
_____
_____

His mother wore _____
_____
_____
_____
_____

Their flowers were _____
_____
_____
_____
_____

Rehearsal Dinner

You Are Invited

Date _____

Time _____

Place _____

Given by _____

_____

Special gifts/tokens _____

_____

_____

_____

_____

Special memories

_____

_____

_____

_____

_____

_____

_____

The Bachelor/Bachelorette Party

Special memories _____

_____

_____

_____

_____

photo

photo

The Morning of the Day

Where did I spend my last night? _____

_____

What time did I get up? _____

What was the weather like? _____

_____

What did I eat? _____

_____

My hair was done by _____
and the style was _____

My makeup was done by _____

Did everything go according to plan? _____

_____

_____

Did I get to church/temple on time? _____

How did I get there? _____

Where did the attendants get ready? _____

_____

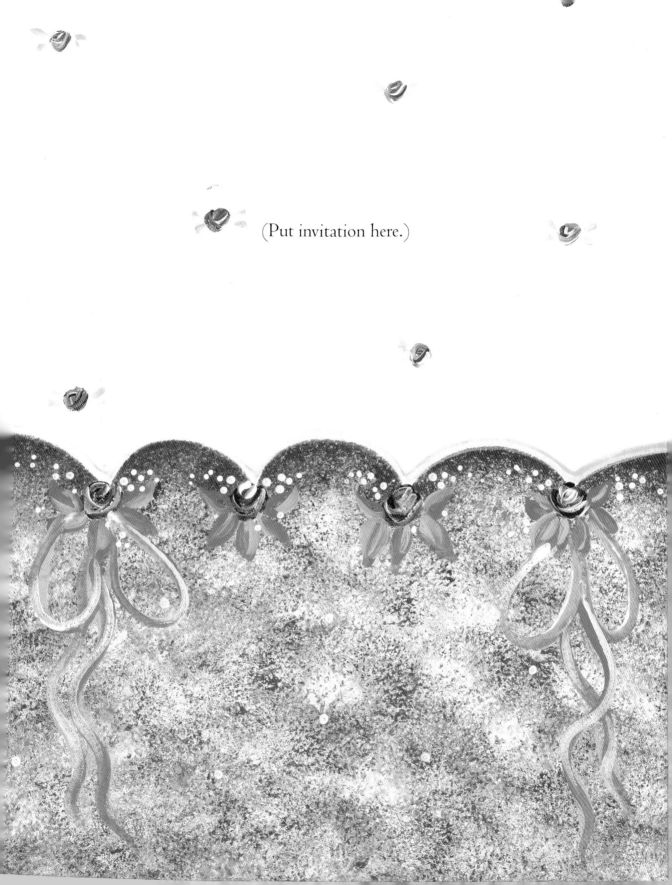

(Put invitation here.)

The Ceremony

Time _____

Order of processional _____

_____

Who gave me away? _____

Who did the readings/intentions and what were they? _____

_____

_____

Who shared the altar with us? _____

_____

_____

Special music _____

_____

The vows we exchanged _____

_____

_____

The rings we exchanged _____

_____

Unplanned moments that made the ceremony very special

_____

_____

_____

Memories of the Special Day

(Place programs and special readings here.)

(Place wedding picture here.)

photo

photo

photo

In ℬetween Time

How did we get from the ceremony to the reception? _____

_____

_____

Did we do anything special? _____

_____

_____

How did our guests get from the ceremony to the reception? _____

_____

_____

photo

photo

photo

photo

The Menu

Cocktail hour _____

_____

Appetizers _____

_____

First course _____

_____

_____

Main course _____

_____

_____

Dessert _____

_____

_____

Caterer _____

_____

Wines/beverages _____

_____

The Wedding Cake

What kind of cake was it? _____
_____

What did it look like? _____
_____

Cake cutting memories _____
_____
_____

The cake was baked by _____
_____

(Place picture of wedding cake here.)

The Reception

Place _____

Time _____

Flowers/decorations _____

_____

_____

_____

_____

Music _____

_____

_____

_____

We danced "Our First Dance" to _____

_____

_____

_____

My father and I danced to _____

_____

His mother and he danced to _____

_____

_____

The first toast _____

_____

_____

_____

_____

_____

_____

_____

Who caught the bouquet? _____

_____

_____

Who caught the garter? _____

_____

_____

_____

Who photographed/video recorded the day? _____

_____

_____

_____

Wishes from *Family* and Friends

Family and Friends
Who Shared Our Day

photo

photo

photo

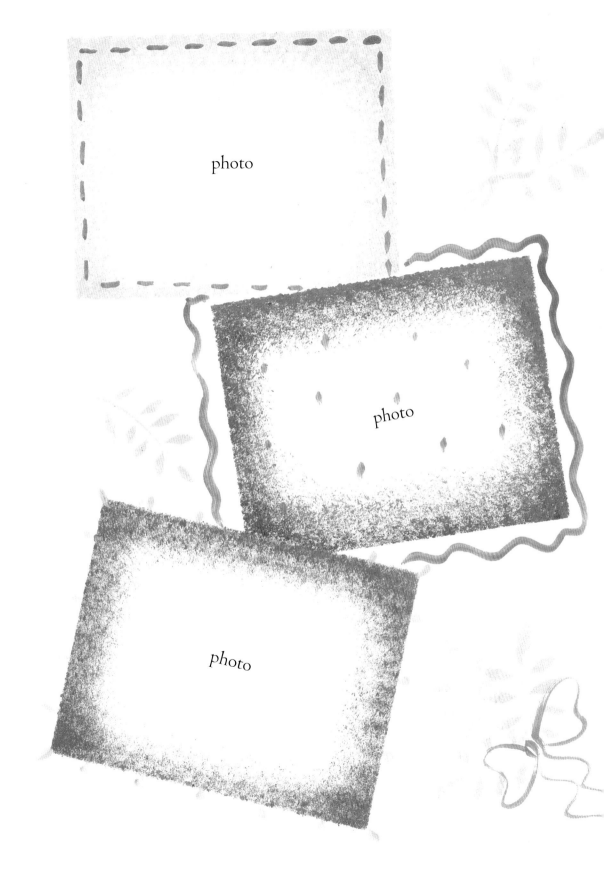

The Celebration Continues

The Wedding Night

What time did we leave the reception? _____

_____

Where did we spend our first night together as husband and wife?

_____

_____

_____

Bride's trousseau _____

_____

_____

_____

Special memories _____

_____

_____

_____

_____

_____

_____

(Place marriage certificate here.)

(Place marriage license here.)

Our Heoneymoon

Where did we go? _____
_____
_____

Where did we stay? _____
_____
_____
_____

We honeymooned from _____
to _____

Favorite places visited _____
_____
_____
_____

Special memories _____
_____
_____
_____

photo

photo

photo

Our $\mathcal{L}$ife Begins

Our new address is _____

_____

_____

_____

Description of our first home _____

_____

_____

_____

_____

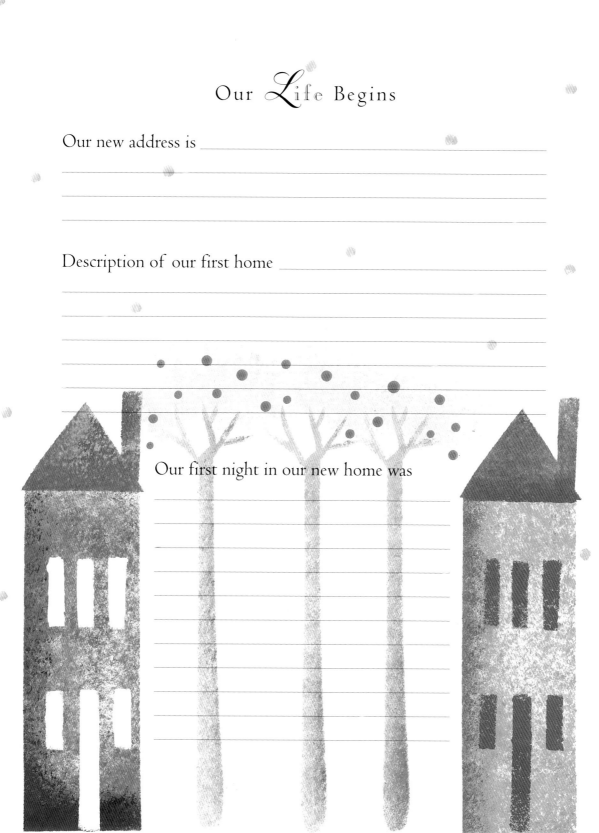

Our first night in our new home was

_____

_____

_____

_____

_____

_____

_____

_____

_____

For Better, For Worse

How has my life changed? _____

_____

_____

_____

_____

_____

_____

_____

What makes me happiest now? _____

_____

_____

_____

_____

_____

_____

_____

What challenges me now? _____
_____
_____
_____
_____
_____
_____
_____

Is being married everything I thought it would be? _____
_____
_____
_____
_____
_____
_____
_____

Moments to Remember

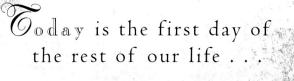

Today is the first day of
the rest of our life . . .